TIDAL WAVES AND FLOODING

© Aladdin Books Ltd 2005

New edition published in the
United States in 2005 by:
Stargazer Books
c/o The Creative Company
123 South Broad Street
P.O. Box 227
Mankato, Minnesota 56002

Designer: Stephen Woosnam-Savage
Editors: Fiona Robertson
          Libby Volke
Picture Researchers: Emma Krikler
                      Brian Hunter Smart
Illustrator: Mike Saunders

Printed in UAE

Library of Congress Cataloging-in-Publication Data

Walker, Jane (Jane Alison)
   Tidal waves and flooding / by Jane Walker. --New ed.
     p. cm.-- (Natural disasters)
   Includes index.
   ISBN 1-932799-62-1 (alk. paper)
     1. Tsunamis--Juvenile literature.
     I. Saunders, Mike. II. Title. III. Series.

GC221.5.W35 2004
363.34'93--dc22

                                   2004041608

Natural Disasters

TIDAL WAVES
AND FLOODING

JANE WALKER

STARGAZER BOOKS

CONTENTS

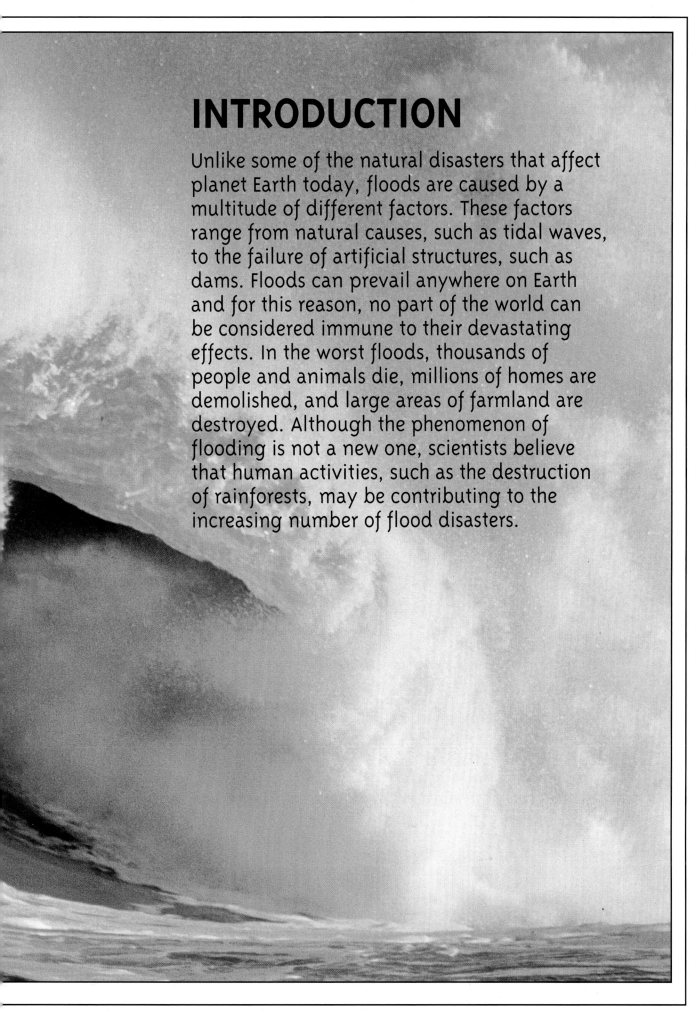

INTRODUCTION

Unlike some of the natural disasters that affect planet Earth today, floods are caused by a multitude of different factors. These factors range from natural causes, such as tidal waves, to the failure of artificial structures, such as dams. Floods can prevail anywhere on Earth and for this reason, no part of the world can be considered immune to their devastating effects. In the worst floods, thousands of people and animals die, millions of homes are demolished, and large areas of farmland are destroyed. Although the phenomenon of flooding is not a new one, scientists believe that human activities, such as the destruction of rainforests, may be contributing to the increasing number of flood disasters.

WHAT ARE FLOODS?

Floods are the waters that cover an area of land that is normally dry. They have affected almost every corner of the earth at some time or another, but those that cause the greatest amount of damage are the result of extreme weather conditions.

Tropical storms, which are called typhoons, hurricanes, or cyclones in different parts of the world, whip up the winds over the oceans and create huge waves. These waves, known as storm surges, race toward the shore and crash onto the coastline. The country of Bangladesh has suffered serious flooding on many occasions. Cyclones in the Bay of Bengal have sent huge waves crashing over the low-lying coastal areas. Other enormous waves that produce severe flooding are the so-called tidal waves, or *tsunamis*, that result from earthquakes or volcanic eruptions.

The millions of tons of rock, soil, and mud unleashed during a landslide can block a river valley or dam, causing water levels to rise dramatically. Flooding can also follow a seiche, the violent movement of lake waters following an earthquake. The most frequent cause, however, is when heavy rains and melting snow and ice make inland rivers and dams burst. This problem is made worse in areas where large numbers of trees have been cleared. Stripped of their vegetation, the hillsides cannot hold the excess water, which runs off and causes flooding in lowland areas.

← During powerful storms, strong winds whip up high waves that crash down on the coastline. Sea defenses are often smashed to pieces, causing serious flooding in areas along the coast and extensive damage to property.

→ Sudden, violent bursts of water surging down narrow mountain valleys or dry riverbeds are called flash floods. These raging torrents of water, such as the one shown right at El Oued in Algeria, can flood an area for just a few hours, or even minutes, before subsiding.

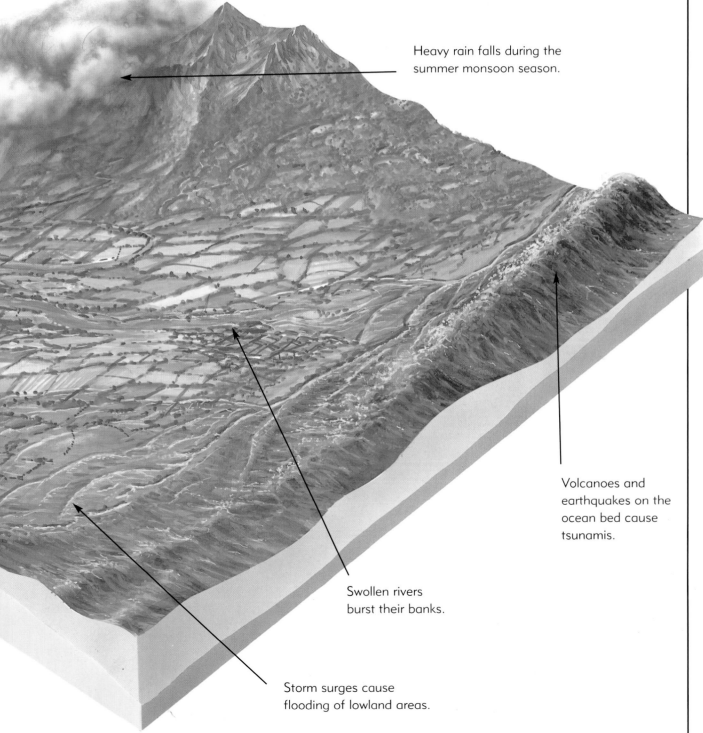

Heavy rain falls during the summer monsoon season.

Volcanoes and earthquakes on the ocean bed cause tsunamis.

Swollen rivers burst their banks.

Storm surges cause flooding of lowland areas.

WHAT IS A TIDAL WAVE?

When an earthquake occurs on the ocean floor, it releases huge amounts of energy in shock waves. The waves travel outward in ripple-like movements called seismic waves. They spread out from the center, or focus, of the earthquake, causing the seabed to jolt and shift. These movements of the seabed create enormous waves that can pass through the seas at speeds of between 390 and 490 miles per hour, depending on the depth of the sea. The waves are called *tsunamis*, after the Japanese word for "storm waves." They are sometimes referred to as "tidal waves," although they have nothing to do with tides.

In deep waters, *tsunamis* are low and wide, often less than 3 ft high and with as much as 90 miles between the crest of one wave and the next. Yet, when the waves reach shallower water, they become more deadly as they rear up to heights of 100 ft or more, and crash inland, causing widespread devastation.

Using special equipment, scientists can predict *tsunamis* in some parts of the world. The Tsunami Warning System in Hawaii monitors seismic activity in the Pacific region.

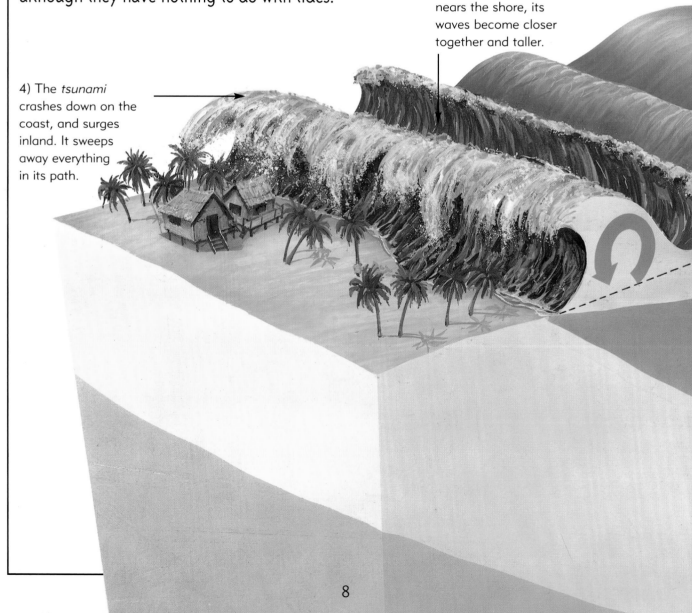

3) When the *tsunami* nears the shore, its waves become closer together and taller.

4) The *tsunami* crashes down on the coast, and surges inland. It sweeps away everything in its path.

Volcanic causes

Tsunamis can also be caused when an underwater volcano or a volcanic island erupts. After the volcanic island of Krakatau exploded in 1883, a *tsunami* 115 ft high smashed into the nearby islands of Java and Sumatra, killing 36,000 people. Ninety percent of all recorded *tsunamis* have been in the Pacific Ocean, where there are over 10,000 volcanoes.

2) The seismic waves make the seabed jolt, which creates huge sea waves.

1) When an earthquake occurs below the ocean floor, part of the seabed is forced upward.

A *tsunami* may strike without warning, often on a calm day. The earthquake that unleashed it probably occurred far away, so the shockwaves would not be felt on land. The largest recorded tsunami (280 ft high) surged past the Japanese island of Ishigaki in 1971. Since 1990, ten major *tsunamis* have killed more than 4,000 people. In 1998, a strong earthquake struck Papua New Guinea, and caused a 23-ft-high *tsunami*. Over 3,000 people drowned.

THE WORLD'S WATER

The world's water supply is constantly circulating around the earth in a process known as the water, or hydrological cycle. Heat from the sun's rays causes some of the water in the world's oceans, lakes, rivers, and streams to evaporate and turn into water vapor. This vapor rises up into the air and condenses to form clouds. The water droplets in the clouds fall back down to Earth as rain or snow, most of which falls into the oceans. About one-tenth falls into streams and rivers on the land, and it is eventually carried back to the oceans.

This natural cycle of water is altered in a number of ways. Storm rains and sudden climatic changes, such as a rise in temperature, result in excess quantities of water that cannot be absorbed by the soil, vegetation, or atmosphere, or channeled in the normal way.

River

Evaporation
Water vapor rises up into the air from the oceans, rivers, and lakes, cools, and then forms clouds.

Ocean

About **98** percent of the water in the water cycle comes from oceans, rivers, lakes, and streams. The remaining 2 percent comes from the water vapor given off by plants, mostly through their leaves. This process is called transpiration.

Transpiration

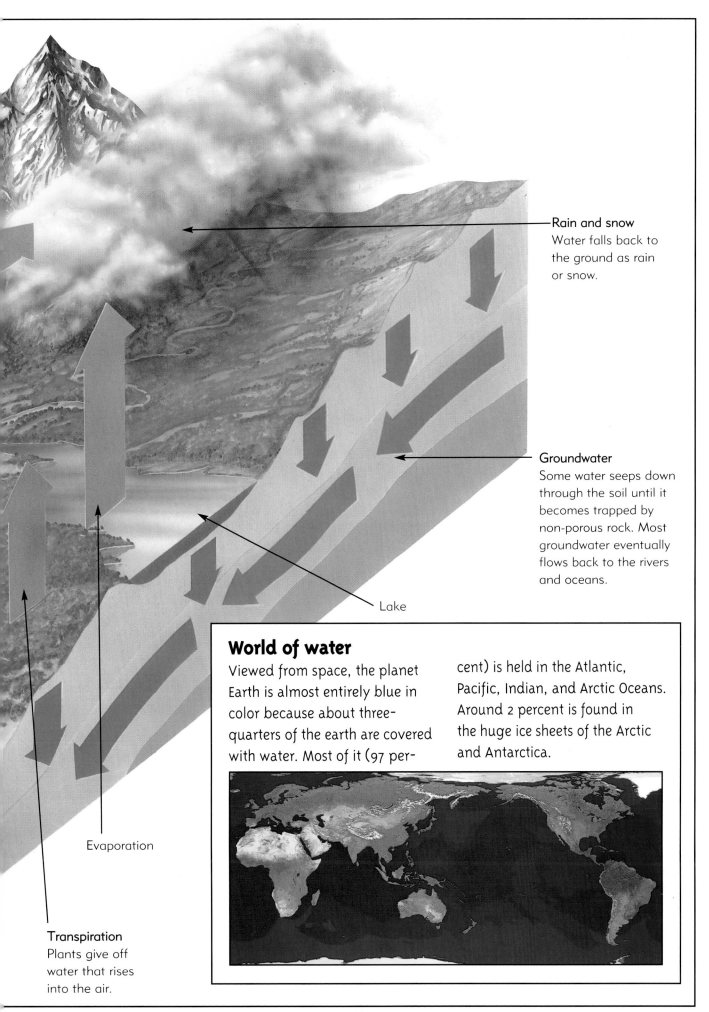

Rain and snow
Water falls back to the ground as rain or snow.

Groundwater
Some water seeps down through the soil until it becomes trapped by non-porous rock. Most groundwater eventually flows back to the rivers and oceans.

Lake

Evaporation

Transpiration
Plants give off water that rises into the air.

World of water

Viewed from space, the planet Earth is almost entirely blue in color because about three-quarters of the earth are covered with water. Most of it (97 percent) is held in the Atlantic, Pacific, Indian, and Arctic Oceans. Around 2 percent is found in the huge ice sheets of the Arctic and Antarctica.

THE AFTER EFFECTS

In the aftermath of a severe flood, thousands of people and animals are found drowned, and whole villages are demolished. Hundreds of thousands of square miles of farmland are ruined as the crops and fertile soil are washed away and replaced by thick mud.

Floods also cause massive destruction of roads, bridges, railroads, and water and power supplies. Rescue workers have difficulty in bringing food and medical supplies to many people trapped by the flood waters. Broken sewers and the lack of clean water can lead to the rapid spread of diseases like cholera.

Between February and April 2000, Mozambique suffered its worst floods for 150 years. Several cyclones and record rains pounded the country, killing 700 people and leaving half a million homeless. In March 2001, further floods forced nearly 200,000 people to evacuate.

↑ People in the Mekong Delta experienced terrible flooding in September 2000.

← Cyclone Elise, Cyclone Hudah, and Tropical Storm Gloria drenched Mozambique in spring 2000, causing widespread homelessness.

→ In 1998, many Asian countries struggled to cope with floods. Half of the city Dhaka, in Bangladesh (right), was under water. The country was struck again in 2000 and 2001. In China, 3,000 people died and 30 million became homeless.

THE FLOODED COAST

Many coastlines suffer from serious flooding, either due to unusually high tides or because the land lies below sea level. In January 1953, winds of over 115 mph combined with the high tide to produce storm surges. Vast areas of fertile land along the North Sea coastline of several countries were flooded. Sea levels reached more than 16 ft above normal, and over 1,800 people were killed.

Most of the population of Bangladesh live in the lowlands of the Ganges Delta on the Bay of Bengal. Despite the high risk of flooding on the tidal lands there, the fertile soil offers the poor of Bangladesh a place to build their homes and to farm. In 1970, the world's greatest sea flood, from a tropical cyclone in the area, left half a million people dead.

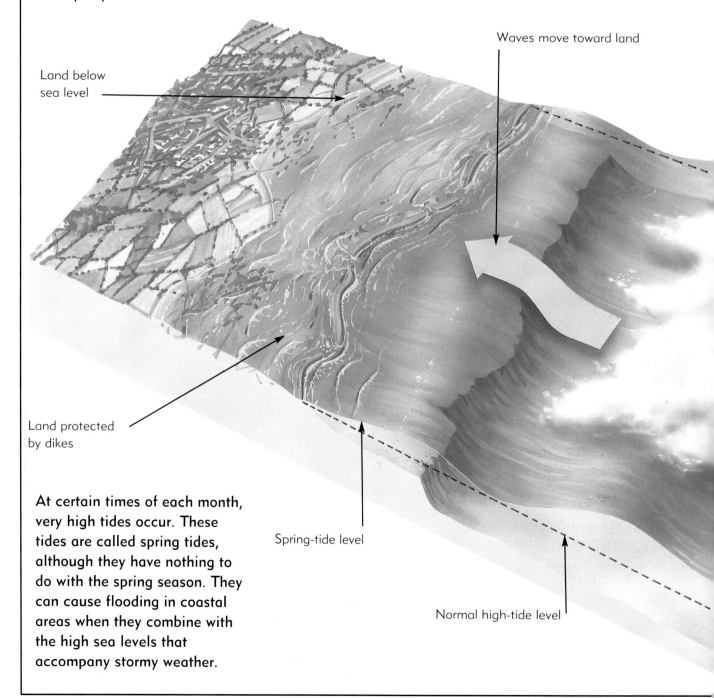

Land below sea level

Waves move toward land

Land protected by dikes

Spring-tide level

Normal high-tide level

At certain times of each month, very high tides occur. These tides are called spring tides, although they have nothing to do with the spring season. They can cause flooding in coastal areas when they combine with the high sea levels that accompany stormy weather.

The Netherlands

Much of the land along the coast of The Netherlands lies below sea level and is known as the polders. Prins Alexander Polder, the lowest in the country, lies nearly 23 ft below sea level. To protect the polders from flooding, huge protective walls called dikes have been built along the coast. These windmills, on a dike in the Kinderdijk region, once drained water from surrounding polders. They are still used in summer, for show.

Stormy weather at sea

→ In December 1999, Venezuela was devastated by its worst floods for 50 years. Raging rivers and mudslides along the Caribbean coast left between 20,000 and 50,000 people dead or missing. The capital, Caracas (shown right), was badly hit, with several shantytowns swept away.

CITIES UNDER THREAT

In the developing world, many cities are built in areas that are prone to regular coastal flooding. In Guayaquil in Ecuador, more than half the population lives in shanty dwellings that suffer from regular sea flooding, in addition to flooding from the nearby Guayas River. Another city built on tidal land is Jakarta in Indonesia, where many of the poor build flimsy, makeshift houses on low-lying land.

Large areas of London, England, including the subway and the docks, are built at, or below, sea level. In January 1953, the Thames River rose by over 3 feet above the spring-tide level, breaking through its protective walls, which are known as embankments, in several places. To avoid the risk of future floods, a tidal flood defense system called the Thames Barrier has been built across the river. The barrier, which was opened in 1984, consists of a wall of ten steel gates. These gates can be closed to prevent flood waters surging upstream.

→ **The gates of the Thames Barrier sit on the riverbed in the open position. When the water level rises, they are rotated by large wheel-like structures so that they are in a vertical position and close the openings between the piers, sealing off the river beyond.**

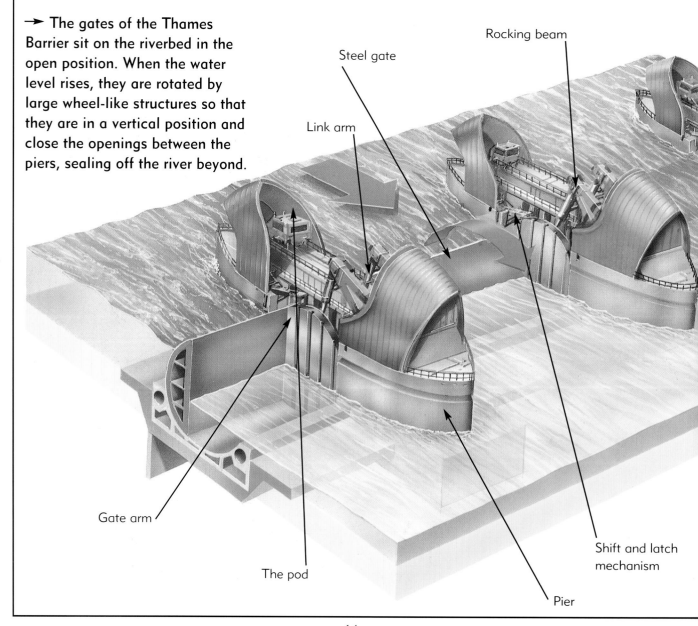

Rocking beam

Steel gate

Link arm

Gate arm

The pod

Shift and latch mechanism

Pier

16

Florence, 1966

In 1966, the Arno River in Italy broke its banks, covering the low-lying districts of Florence in about 19 ft of mud and water. The flood waters surged through the streets so rapidly that thousands of people were stranded in the top floors of their homes. Many priceless art treasures were destroyed or damaged.

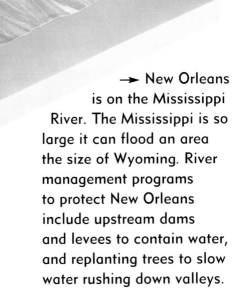

→ New Orleans is on the Mississippi River. The Mississippi is so large it can flood an area the size of Wyoming. River management programs to protect New Orleans include upstream dams and levees to contain water, and replanting trees to slow water rushing down valleys.

RIVER FLOODS

Rivers are responsible for more floods than lakes or seas. Many rivers overflow their banks once or twice each year, often during the spring months. A river may flood when large amounts of ice and snow on nearby hills and mountains suddenly melt. The frozen ground cannot soak up the extra water, and the rapid thaw causes severe flooding. Another reason is too much rain falling within a short period of time. Asian rivers often flood after the heavy rains of the monsoon season. The calm river waters swell with the extra water, and turn into raging muddy torrents.

For centuries, snow melts from the Alps have caused the Po River to flood through Northern Italy. The nutrients carried down in the flood waters from the mountains have made this area extremely fertile. However, these flood waters are also causing the city of Venice to sink farther below the water level each year.

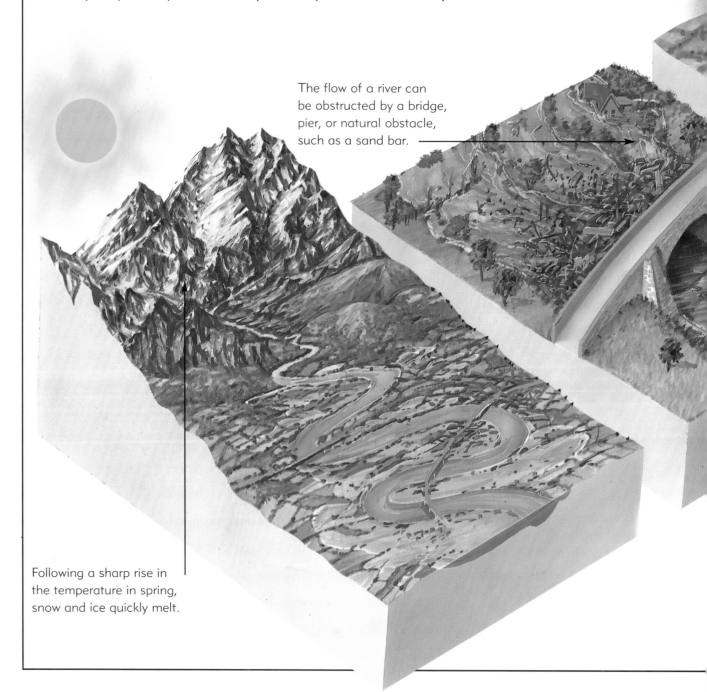

The flow of a river can be obstructed by a bridge, pier, or natural obstacle, such as a sand bar.

Following a sharp rise in the temperature in spring, snow and ice quickly melt.

A river channel is a hollowed-out passageway made by flowing water. The size and position of the channel change as the flow of water erodes one part of the bank, and builds up another.

Torrential rain quickly soaks into the land until the soil cannot hold any more water.

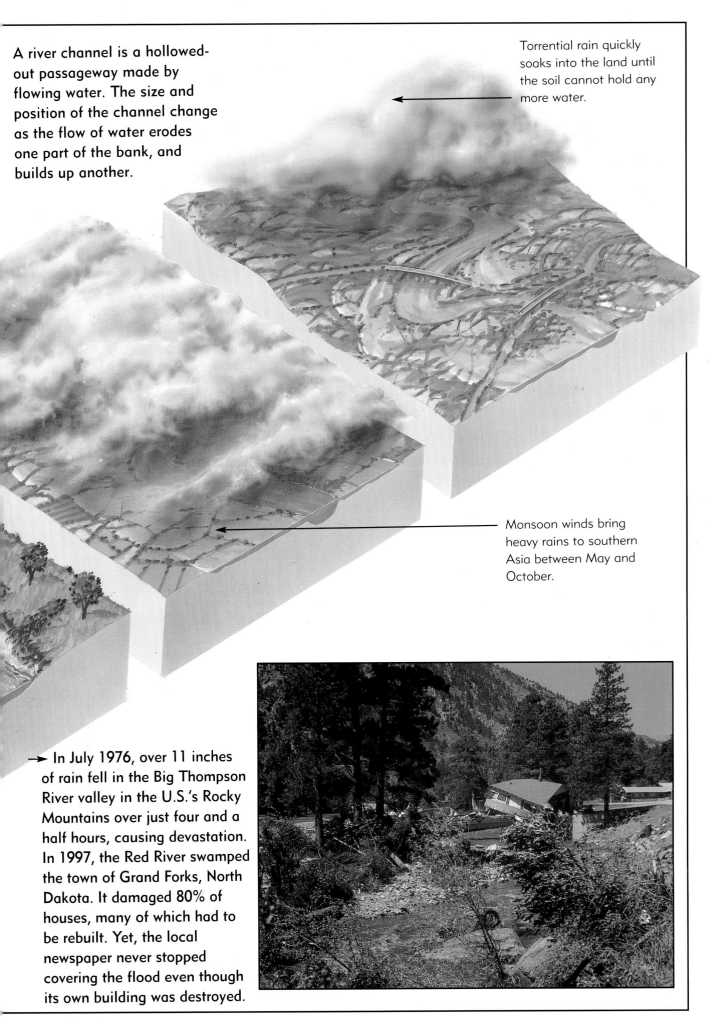

Monsoon winds bring heavy rains to southern Asia between May and October.

→ In July 1976, over 11 inches of rain fell in the Big Thompson River valley in the U.S.'s Rocky Mountains over just four and a half hours, causing devastation. In 1997, the Red River swamped the town of Grand Forks, North Dakota. It damaged 80% of houses, many of which had to be rebuilt. Yet, the local newspaper never stopped covering the flood even though its own building was destroyed.

THE GREAT RIVERS

China's Huang He, or Yellow River, has flooded over 1,500 times during the past 3,500 years. It has claimed more lives than any other feature on the earth's surface, earning itself the nickname "China's Sorrow." In 1887, the river was responsible for one of the world's worst natural disasters. An estimated 900,000 people died, and at least one million more perished in the aftermath of starvation and disease. Over 50,000 square miles of land was flooded, and more than two million people lost their homes.

In the fight to control the Huang He, the Chinese have built a system of protective dikes, up to 98 ft thick at their base in places. They line the dikes with kaoliang, a wheatlike plant whose thick, clumpy roots are bound together tightly in huge bales. The root fibers retain much of the silt carried by the river and so prevent erosion of the river bank.

The vast Mississippi River system in North America drains an area that covers 31 American states and two Canadian provinces. At one time, the land around the lower Mississippi was considered to be one of the world's most dangerous flood areas. Floods in 1927, which threatened to destroy the city of New Orleans, killed a total of 246 people and forced 650,000 to evacuate their homes.

In 1927, the Mississippi River flooded an area of almost 17 million acres. The flood waters caused extensive damage in many cities and towns, including the city of Memphis (below).

A river picks up material as it flows quickly through the hills. It later deposits a mixture of rocks and soil, called sediment, when it passes more slowly through the flat lowlands, on its way out to sea. When a river floods, the land on either side of its banks is covered in water. This land is called the floodplain. Floodplains help prevent further flooding as they can store a large amount of water. When the river level drops, its waters can once again be contained within the river channel.

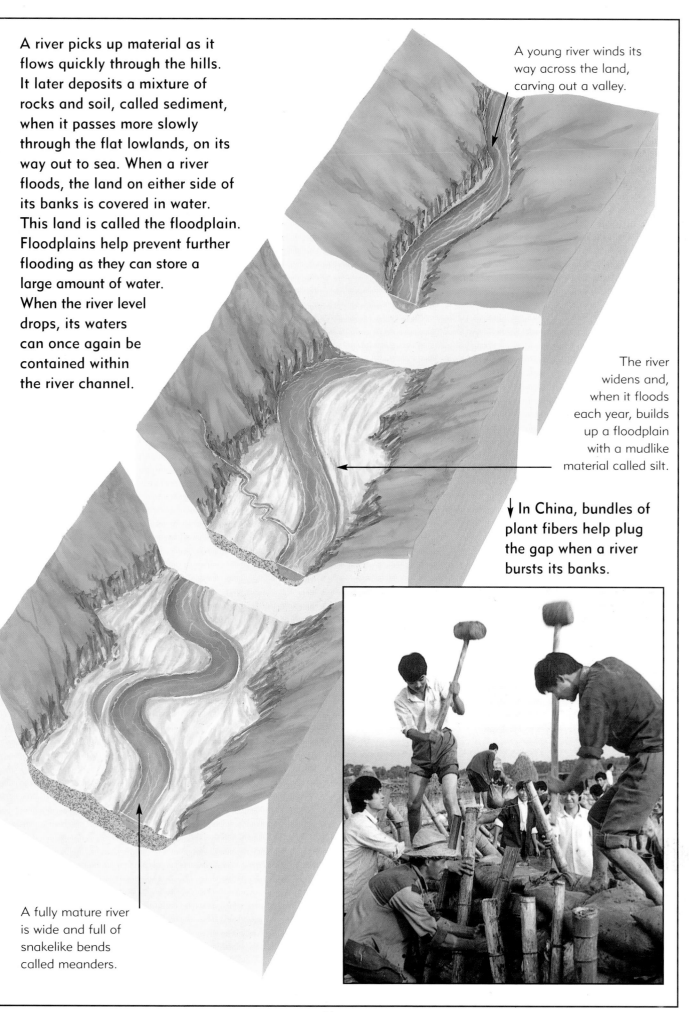

A young river winds its way across the land, carving out a valley.

The river widens and, when it floods each year, builds up a floodplain with a mudlike material called silt.

↓ In China, bundles of plant fibers help plug the gap when a river bursts its banks.

A fully mature river is wide and full of snakelike bends called meanders.

FLOODS IN HISTORY

Throughout history, floods have had a major impact on people and their surroundings. One of the most famous flood legends is the story of Noah and his Ark from the Old Testament. After 40 days of heavy rains, the whole Earth was flooded. So, Noah and his family took refuge in a huge wooden boat, together with dozens of different animals, until the waters subsided.

In Greek literature, the story about the flood of Deucalion is very similar to that of Noah's Ark. Deucalion was the father of Hellen, ancestor of the Hellenic race. Legend has it that Zeus, king of the Greek gods, was so disgusted with the behavior of mankind that he created a flood. Deucalion, however, had built a boat that he and his wife drifted in during the nine days of the flood.

According to the North American Indians, the spring floods were caused by a mouse chewing a hole in a bag that contained the sun's rays. The heat escaped through the hole and melted the winter snows.

The Arno River in Italy regularly floods the area around the city of Florence. The first recorded flood there dates back to the 2nd century AD.

← The carving on this 12th-century altar in an Austrian convent depicts the dove returning to Noah's Ark. In the story of Noah, flood waters were said to have covered the whole Earth. It is believed that the flood occurred around 3200 BC. In 1929, archeologists discovered evidence of a major flood by the Euphrates River in Mesopotamia (modern Iraq). The extent of it was so great that some historians believe it may have been the origin of the Noah's flood story.

↓ When the Yangtze River in China broke its banks in 1931, the river's waters rose some 98 ft above their normal level. They flooded the surrounding plains where almost half of the country's principal food crop, rice, is grown. The city of Hankou (below) was one of those affected by the flood waters. Over 3.5 million people died, either from drowning or from famine.

Da Vinci's plans to stop flooding

Leonardo da Vinci was a great engineer, architect, and artist who lived in Italy in the 16th century. He drew up plans for a flood-control system on the Arno River. His designs included a large basin to store excess water, a canal, and floodgates to bring the river under control, all of which were later rejected.

THE GOOD AND THE BAD

The impact of a serious flood goes well beyond the large numbers of human casualties and destroyed homes that occur in its immediate aftermath. A huge clearing-up operation is needed to remove the thousands of tons of mud and debris that are deposited in the stricken area. Broken water pipes may result in contaminated water supplies, leading to outbreaks of diseases such as cholera, typhoid, and dysentery. In the densely populated countries of the developing world, the destruction of food crops and livestock can cause a major famine.

However, in certain parts of the world, flooding does bring benefits. In Egypt, the annual floods of the Nile River have deposited rich, fertile sediments around the Nile Delta for thousands of years. However, since the Aswan Dam was built in the south of Egypt in the 1960s, much of these fertile deposits have remained trapped on the bed of Lake Nasser. Egyptian farmers now have to import expensive chemical fertilizers from abroad to use on their land.

3) After the flood waters subsided, millions of tons of fertile sediment were left on the land.

1) Without rain, no crops will grow on the dry land beside the Nile.

2) The Nile's flood waters covered the delta lands between August and October.

The Nile
The annual top-up of nutrient-rich soil on the delta plains of the Nile River once made the soil here the most fertile in the world.

→ Further damage to both land and property results from soil erosion (shown right), when the raging torrent of flood waters carry away the surrounding topsoil. The problem is worse where large areas of trees have been cleared, either for cultivation or for building. The vegetation acts like a sponge, soaking up the excess water. If it is removed, the soil cannot absorb large amounts of water, so it simply runs off the land, causing flooding in lowland areas.

4) In the later summer, the farmers planted their crops.

Growing crops on floodlands

The floodplains that build up each time a river floods provide perfect land for growing a crop such as rice. In the delta areas of the Mekong River in Vietnam and the Ganges River in India, farmers build protective walls to keep their paddy fields continually flooded (illustrated far right). Rice, the staple food crop of these regions, would be unable to thrive without the mineral and organic deposits that are found in the flood waters.

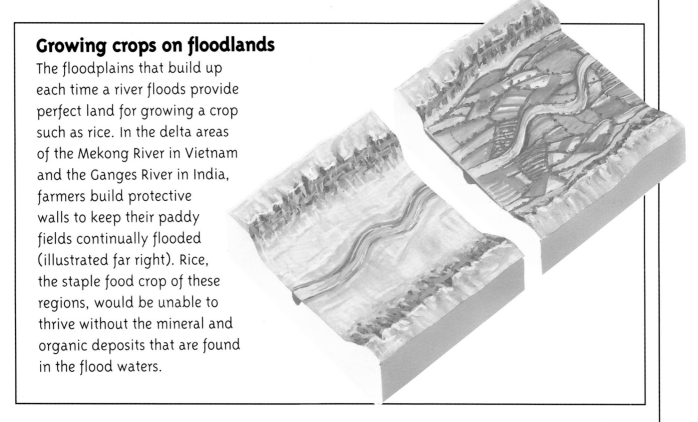

ARE WE CAUSING MORE?

In many areas of the world, more and more land is being cleared of trees and other vegetation. This deforestation provides much needed farmland on which to produce food for the world's growing population. But it also causes soil erosion, with a greater risk of lowland flooding. Severe flooding in Mexico in 1998 was blamed in part on the tree-felling activities in the region.

Deforestation, together with the burning of fossil fuels and trees, increases the amount of carbon dioxide in the atmosphere. Carbon dioxide is a greenhouse gas, which means that it helps to trap enough heat close to the earth's surface for life to survive. However, if the amount of greenhouse gases in the atmosphere increases because of pollution or the burning of fossil fuels, temperatures around the world could rise. Increases of between 1.5 and 2.5 degrees Fahrenheit could lead to climate changes.

Power plants and factories burn fossil fuels that produce greenhouse gases.

Rising sea levels

Scientists are worried that the slow but steady increase in the world's temperatures might make the world's ice sheets and glaciers begin to melt, raising sea levels across the world. At present, they estimate that the sea level is rising by about 1 to 2 mm each year. If this trend were to continue, low-lying countries could be left permanently under water.

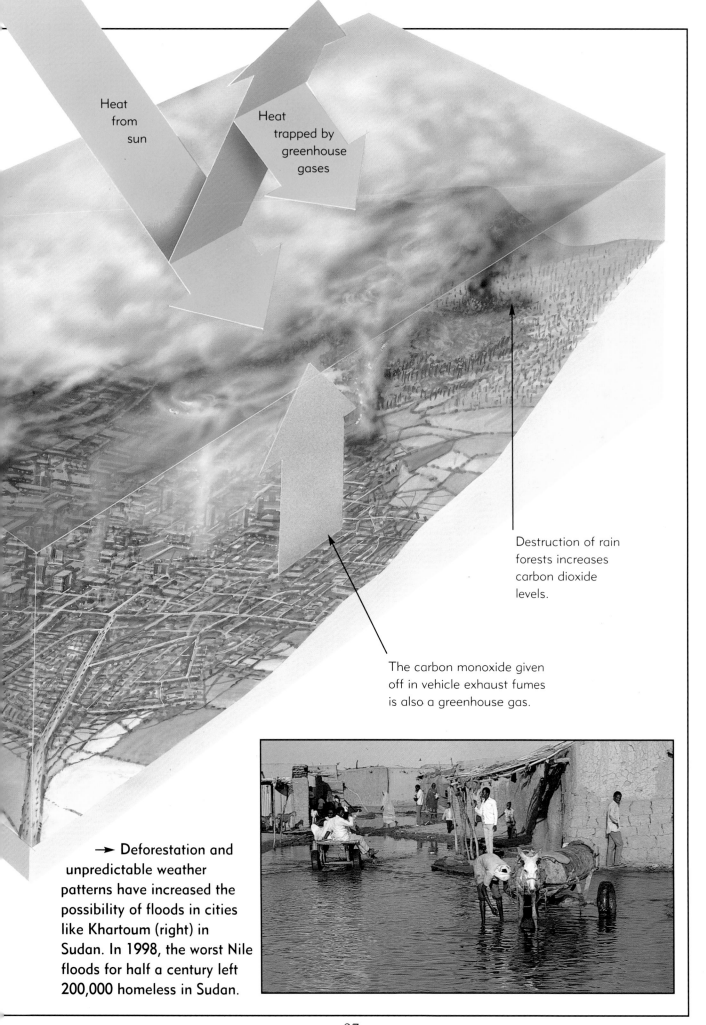

Heat from sun

Heat trapped by greenhouse gases

Destruction of rain forests increases carbon dioxide levels.

The carbon monoxide given off in vehicle exhaust fumes is also a greenhouse gas.

→ Deforestation and unpredictable weather patterns have increased the possibility of floods in cities like Khartoum (right) in Sudan. In 1998, the worst Nile floods for half a century left 200,000 homeless in Sudan.

WHAT CAN WE DO?

Although floods can never be prevented, a variety of measures can be adopted to reduce their devastating impact. Improved warning and evacuation systems will ensure that fewer casualties occur. River levels are constantly monitored by the U.S. National Weather Service, which uses radar to predict the time, place, and amount of future rain and snow falls.

The Indian government is encouraging the replanting of trees in the Himalayas. This reforestation will provide people with firewood and will also keep enough trees growing to prevent the run-off of heavy rains. On a worldwide scale, slowing the rate of deforestation, and using alternative, cleaner sources of power, such as solar, wind, and wave power, can help reduce carbon dioxide levels.

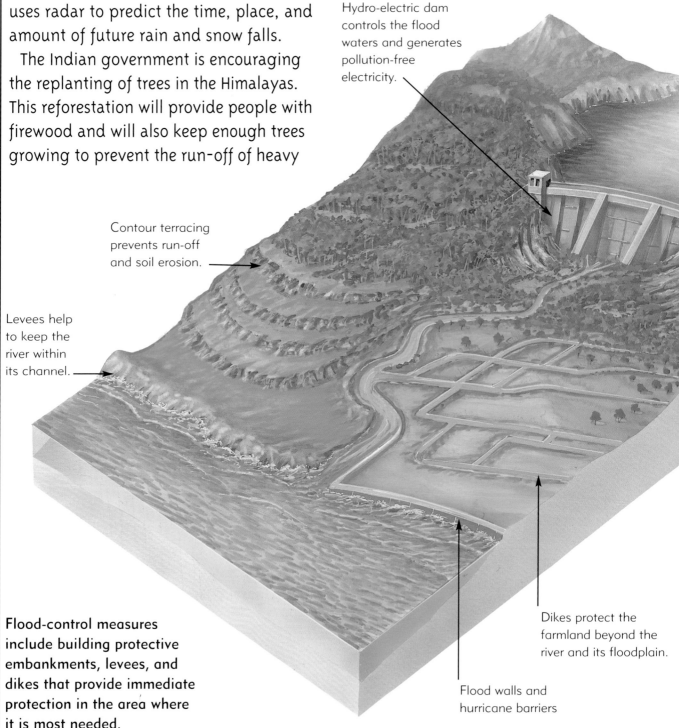

Hydro-electric dam controls the flood waters and generates pollution-free electricity.

Contour terracing prevents run-off and soil erosion.

Levees help to keep the river within its channel.

Dikes protect the farmland beyond the river and its floodplain.

Flood walls and hurricane barriers

Flood-control measures include building protective embankments, levees, and dikes that provide immediate protection in the area where it is most needed.

→ Large-scale contour terracing of the steep hills on either side of a river, traps rainwater in the soil and vegetation. Contour terracing, as seen in these rice terraces in the Philippines, also prevents soil erosion. When fertile topsoil is washed down into the river, it is deposited as silt on the riverbed. This causes the height of the river bed to increase, making the river more prone to flooding.

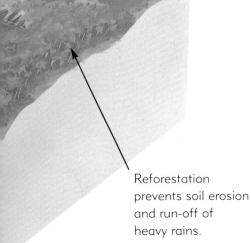

Reforestation prevents soil erosion and run-off of heavy rains.

Preventive measures

One method of flood prevention is to reinforce coastal defenses with huge slabs of concrete linked together. This system is used in Japan (right). For countries that are prone to flooding, special shelters can be built. Bangladesh has 63 such shelters. They are raised 12 feet above the ground. Over 350,000 people sought refuge in them from the flooding caused by the 1991 cylone in that area.

FACT FILE

The world's water

The world's total water supply is 326 million cubic miles. 97 percent of this is held in the oceans. Icecaps and glaciers, including the Arctic and Antarctic ice sheets, contain 7 million cubic miles of water. Seventy percent of the world's freshwater supply is in a frozen state. Less than 1 percent of the world's total water supply is involved in the water cycle at any given time.

Tsunamis

Some *tsunamis* contain so much water that they flood up to a mile inland. Since 1819, over 100 *tsunamis* have reached the shores of Hawaii. A *tsunami* measuring at least 25 ft is recorded along the Japanese coastline every 15 years.

Tsunami warnings

Scientists in Hawaii have developed a *tsunami* detection system that uses sonic devices on the ocean floor to send news of underwater quakes to computers on land, via satellites.

RECENT *TSUNAMIS*

1998

Papua New Guinea—3,000 people died after a *tsunami* completely washed away the villages of Arop and Warapu, and devastated most of Sissano and Malol.

2001

Peru—In June, the Peruvian coast was hit by a *tsunami* 22 ft high, that surged 1/2 mile inland and destroyed hundreds of homes.

Twenty-six people died and 76 are still missing.

2002

Honduras—Ten-foot-high waves battered the coast in September, destroying hundreds of homes and displacing 1,700 people.

Floods in the future

As a result of global warming, temperatures are expected to rise by 3–9°F in the next century. If sea levels rise by three feet by the year 2030, as some scientists have predicted, 15 million Bangladeshis could be left homeless. Cities such as London, Tokyo, Shanghai, Rome, and Rio de Janeiro may also be at risk.

FLOOD FACTS

Most people killed by a flood

900,000 people died when the Huang He, China, burst its banks in October 1887.

Most damage caused by a flood

890,000 dwellings were destroyed when the Hwai and Yangtze Rivers in eastern China flooded in 1950.

RECENT FLOODS

2000

Mozambique—Floods in the spring killed 700 and left half a million homeless. After the floodwaters receded, people were at risk from landmines washed into new positions by the floods.

Vietnam and Cambodia—1.9 million people were affected by floods along the Mekong River during the monsoon season.

India and Bangladesh—Torrential monsoon rains in the

neighboring countries left 20 million people homeless by October. Over a quarter of Bangladesh was under water.

2001

India—In July, 200,000 people fled their homes, following terrible monsoon rains. This disaster occurred just 2 years after a devastating cyclone struck the area, killing 11,000 people.

China—In July, a massive flash flood drowned 30 people. Just 40 minutes of torrential rain triggered what was China's most ferocious flood for 100 years.

Iran—Flash floods also destroyed areas of northeast Iran in August. 37,000 acres of farmland were underwater after the area's worst flood for 200 years.

2002

Central Europe—In August, severe floods and landslides killed over 100 people from Germany and Austria, to Russia's Black Sea. Nearly 60 people were killed at a resort on the Black Sea.

China—In the worst flooding in a decade, over 2,000 people died, many as a result of landslides made worse by deforestation.

2003

Sri Lanka—In May, torrential rains hit overnight, swamping 350,000 homes under 9 ft of water. 260 were confirmed dead, 500 are missing.

France—27,000 people were evacuated around the city of Arles in December. The torrential rain, which fell at a rate of 4 inches in just 24 hrs, claimed six lives.

GLOSSARY

atmosphere—the layer of gases that surrounds the earth.

carbon dioxide—one of the gases found naturally in the atmosphere. It is also produced by burning fossil fuels.

channel—the sides and bottom of a river, inside which the water is normally stored.

condense—when a gas cools and turns into a liquid.

deforestation—the removal of large numbers of trees from the landscape.

dike—a protective wall, usually built of earth reinforced with stone, that keeps water away from farmland.

earthquake—a violent shaking movement in the earth's crust that releases huge amounts of energy.

embankment—a wall built along the banks of a river to prevent it from flooding.

evaporate—when a liquid is heated and turns into a vapor.

fertile—suitable for growing healthy crops.

flash flood—a sudden torrent of water that sweeps over dry land. It is usually caused by a heavy rainstorm.

floodplain—the land on either side of a river that is covered with water when the river bursts its banks.

greenhouse gas—a gas in the atmosphere that traps the sun's heat and keeps the earth warm.

hurricane—a spinning tropical storm that occurs over the Atlantic Ocean.

hydrologist—a scientist who studies the movement of water on, below, and above the earth's surface.

levee—a bank beside a river that prevents the river's water from spilling onto the land.

monsoon—a seasonal wind that blows in Asia and brings very heavy rain during the summer.

polder—a low-lying area where the water has been drained away and the land reclaimed.

reforestation—large-scale replanting of trees in an area that has been deforested.

sediment—a mixture of rock and soil that is carried along by a river.

shock wave—a wave of energy that is released from the center of an earthquake.

silt—a mudlike material made from tiny pieces of rock. Silt is a type of sediment.

soil erosion—the removal of soil by heavy rains and wind.

storm surge—a series of huge sea waves that are whipped up by a tropical storm.

transpiration—the process of plants giving off water vapor through their leaves.

tsunami—huge sea waves caused by shock waves from an earthquake or volcano.

typhoon—a tropical storm in the Far East.

water cycle—the continuous movement of water from the oceans, up through the air to the clouds, and back down to earth as either rain or snow.

INDEX

Photocredits

Abbreviations: l-left, r-right, b-bottom, t-top, c-center, m-middle
Front cover r, back cover — Corbis. Front cover l — Corbis Royalty Free. 3, 19, 21, 26 — Frank Spooner Pictures. 4-5 — Spectrum Colour Library. 6 — Topham Picture Source. 7 — Robert Harding Picture Library. 9 — Roger Ressmeyer/CORBIS. 11 — Science Photo Library. 12l — Noël Quidu/Frank Spooner Pictures. 12mr — Caroline Penn/CORBIS. 13 — Chip Hires/Frank Spooner Pictures. 15t — Paul Almasy/CORBIS. 15br — Rex Features Ltd. 17t, 25 — Frank Lane Picture Library. 17br — Richard Cummins/CORBIS. 20 both — Mary Evans Picture Library. 22 — Ancient Art and Achitecture Collection. 23 both — Poperfoto. 27 — Panos Pictures. 29t — Robert Harding Picture Library. 29b — Environmental Picture Library.